Looking for Cazabon
Lawrence Scott

PAPILLOTE PRESS

London and Trafalgar, Dominica

First published by Papillote Press 2024 in Great Britain

Copyright © Lawrence Scott

Printed by CMP, Poole, Dorset, UK

Book and cover design by Andy Dark

ISBN: 978-1-7391303-6-7

'Looking for Cazabon' has been produced by Papillote People's Press, a book
production enterprise under the Papillote Press imprint.

Papillote Press
23 Rozel Road,
London SW4 0EY,
United Kingdom
And Trafalgar, Dominica
www.papillotepress.co.uk

For Jenny
&
Remembering Derek Walcott

"I sensed, over the years, as a surveyor, that the landscape possessed resonance. The landscape possessed a life, because, the landscape, for me, is like an open book, and the alphabet with which one worked was all around me. But it takes some time to really grasp what this alphabet is, and what the book of the living landscape is..."

WILSON HARRIS, *"The Music of Living Landscape"*

"I hoped that both disciplines might
by painful accretion cohere
and finally ignite ..."

DEREK WALCOTT, "ANOTHER LIFE," CHAPTER 9, II.

CONTENTS

Other books by Lawrence Scott

Novels
Dangerous Freedom
Light Falling on Bamboo
Night Calypso
Aelred's Sin
Witchbroom

Short Stories
Leaving by Plane Swimming back Underwater
Ballad for the New World

Non-fiction
Golconda Our Voices Our Lives

Some of these poems have been published at times in different forms, in the following collections: "Martiniquian Jazz" in the 20th edition of the *Temps des Poètes*, Guadeloupe, 2019; "Boissiere Village", originally i in a series of poems with "Long Circular St James", originally ii, "Stillness", originally iii, and "By the Pool", originally iv, in *Wasafiri*, 25th Anniversary issue, vol 24, issue 59, p33, Autumn 2009; "Tongues", originally "On The Tongue" and a series of poems under "Hingwan Style", two of which were Mayaro 1 & 2 and "Kernahan", originally "Afterthought", in *Agenda*, vol 39, nos 1-3, Winter 2002-2003. These latter poems were also published in Cross Cultures 60, Rodopi Amsterdam-New York, 2002; with "Tongues" originally "Last August". There was also a first publication of some of these in a collection called "Last August," *Trinidad & Tobago Review*, 1995.

Preface

In 2006 I returned home to Trinidad from London to live for three years in order to research the life and times of Michel Jean Cazabon, Trinidad's most famous 19th-century painter. This research led to and concluded with the writing of my novel, *Light Falling on Bamboo*. As I searched for any paintings of Cazabon I could find in both public and private collections, I kept a number of notebooks which chronicled my research, both of the paintings and the landscapes in which he painted.

These research journeys began in Trinidad, discovering where he had painted, often in the intimate walkways of Port of Spain and on the west and south coast, others along the east and north coast of Trinidad, in the foothills of what are the beginning of the Andes – Trinidad is just eight miles or so off Venezuela. The highest mountains you see from Port of Spain are on the east coast of Venezuela. Journeys also took me to Georgetown, Guyana, where Cazabon travelled with the Martiniquan photographer Hippolyte Hartmann for the paintings of what became his Demerara Album; another voyage was to Martinique where he lived in Saint Pierre for eight years. The paintings completed there became Cazabon's Album Martiniquaise.

At this time I was writing sonnet-like poems in my notebook. They were written spontaneously as I began my novel, and seemed a sideways look, or subliminal index to my main work, a glance at Cazabon and his *les paysages*; particularly the effect of the landscape on my thoughts and feelings. This was like the art work which Cezanne called "realisation", which he linked to his personal experiences and "sensations".

While Derek Walcott, in *Another Life*, expressed the hope that the art of poetry and painting might "cohere," I began to hope that my writing of prose might "cohere" in some way with the writing of poetry, each influencing the other. I once showed Walcott some of these sonnets. I remember him saying that I should continue with the sonnet form and build them into a series. They came to represent a sort of random narrative. The writing of prose and poetry began to influence and ignite each other. Much later, I gave the collection this present shape.

One of the crucial aspects of my research had been to learn about painting and the skills required by the artist. I am not a painter and have not ever had a training in art. When I look at the sonnets, they seem to me to be part of my learning to write about landscape and about landscape painting, particularly water-colours, almost like random sketches as I worked on my novel.

The rendering of landscape as word has been a notable aspect of the descriptions in my previous novels and short stories, and Wilson Harris's perception of landscape as providing an "alphabet" as quoted in my epigraph, had already begun to influence how I thought about the employment of landscape in writing, as more than backdrop or context, but as something almost a living character.

As I reflected on the choice of the sonnet form, I saw that it gave me that very precise shape, which reflected Cazabon's principal medium, his small watercolour paintings. I then began to alter their structure with line-spacing and enjambment where

I felt I wanted to signal change and disruption.

Cazabon returned home from Paris in 1848 where he had trained, leaving his wife Louise and three children, including his son Louis Michel, nicknamed Wap. They were reunited in 1852 when he went back to Paris, and then returning to Trinidad together as a family in 1854. My partner, Jenny Green, and I were separated from time to time during my period of research and writing, she in London and then reuniting in Trinidad with further travel elsewhere, to Martinique and Guyana, together for research. This helped me to understand some of the tensions which might have existed for Cazabon in his separations from his wife and children.

I think my poems, like Cazabon's water-colours, attempt a geography of home at a particular time, as I myself arrived back from London and began to write a fiction of his life, caught between here, there and elsewhere through the migrating day as Jenny and I began to visit many of the sites of his paintings in order to compare the contemporary with the 19th century.

Each morning began with what I called the migrating day, parrots in their multitudes, crossing the skies from one side of Port of Spain's Savannah in the early morning to the other side of the city in the west to forage, and then returning again in the evening; hence the long poem, *The Migrating Day* is included as a reflection on the landscape in the same period, but written in a different form; a free verse, long poem.

Lawrence Scott

1

After Cazabon:
On The road

i

Day-moon as white as bone in sheer cobalt
in stinging dry season heat waxing
as afternoon sunlight lasts: I exult
with the smell of earth. Dry leaves quicken
memory, like bush fire in bois canot,
bamboo; seasonal pages, curled parchment.
An archive of barefoot childhood grows
where I dip down beneath flamboyante's
umbrella-flame as afternoon lingers
over the tinted, grey gulf like a flat slate.
The green-blue alchemy of the swamp stirs
light as an artist's oils on his palette:
watercolours, lithographs by Cazabon;
Tristes tropiques in albums with Hartmann.

The Indian laburnum hangs its lanterns
out into the afternoon sun; a drizzle
falling gently through the pouis and palms;
dry season mixed with the coming rains.
The scorched earth yields the green while
wounds weep from the serrated hills
and in the skies dark thunderheads
become cumuli safaris. Cloud caravans
roll out over the gulf to the islands:
Craig, Caledonia, Rock and Lenagan
and one, Pelican, for the pelicans
which soar and swoop;
               all this in an afternoon,
while I wait for your call to startle me
with a voice at once familiar and new.

iii

The Five Islands graze the sunset this evening
like whales on their way to Venezuela:
saffron and blue, a green undulating
gulf-light, a water-colourist's palette; a
poet's metaphor, rhyme, rhythm, metre.
He's painting light as day leans into night.
A moon awaits its stage-cue to enter.
An aura bestowing another kind of light
calls forth awe as palms bow, clouds are stilled.
The music of the spheres are the first stars
stunning us into a silence as we are tuned
into the music as the tropical night jars.
We think we hunger for harmonious sound
till the croaks and pings of frogs resound.

iv

The foreday morning broke through the sea-mist
in the distance beyond Saut d'Eau Island.
It was just him and his brushes, the bush ticking,
the engine of the cigale screaming in staccatos,
the parrots hysterical with their morning flight
in pairs across the hills, the wide valley
of Diego Martin. He remembered an early painting
of the valley tucked away in some portfolio,
hidden in some album. His easel was now set in the bush
at the edge of the cliff looking over the precipice.
The bell bird's toll echoed in the dark valley.
The sea was as flat as a slate, then, crinkling galvanize.
This was a sketch for a lithograph saved in sepia;
the light changing rapidly and imperceptibly.

V

Each time he looked up there was more brightness.
How to catch it before it vanished?
How to catch you, dou dou, darling?
His hand moved constantly: drawing, dabbing,
hovering, hesitant, and then, suddenly,
intent upon its conclusions. As he held
his brush up to measure scale, he sat back
and viewed the sketch from a distance,
tempted then to thinking it completed.
He was already imagining the lithographic
process in Paris. He put that out of his mind;
just him and his island with its light.
Only later would he send it to Cicéri
for him to rub on stone, perform his alchemy.

What did they call it, an impression, an *étude*?
What was the word? Impressionism?
He put that out of his mind. *Just paint, boy,*
listen to Louise; she had his interests at heart.
Wap, get the acid and gum arabic ready.
Michel Jean worked, forgetting where he was,
as in each painting he reclaimed his home.
I leave you? So, I come back. Always like
I just come back, he said to himself as he speckled
the bushes, croton hues. He captured the balata tree,
in the foreground, the razor grass, gri-gri palms,
cashew tree and the young cedar, then
the taller bois canot and the gommier;
the silk-cotton in the deep of the forest.

vii

The slate-grey sea was beginning to shine through
into a blue, not quite cobalt. The sea rippled,
widening around the islands, breaking on the rocks;
the surf scalloping the shoreline. Below
were the red-dirt cliffs hung with lianas,
where sloops with Dutch sails were becalmed
in the vale of light. A fisherman's pirogue
nudged the edges of the fleet. From the depth
the gulls rose, keening into the sky,
their cries the metallic sound of a spoon
scraped on an enamel cup. He imagined
the scene bathed in sepia. *Forget lithographs*,
he said to himself, *paint what you see*.
All he ever tried to paint was the light.

2

On The Coast

Discovery Bay
Down Cedros

Tide in: now that Colón has come and gone
we are left with history books and this time
when driftwood is caught with a tangled seine
in the snare of the mangrove and clogged slime.

At Fullarton the fishing boats creak.
No fish! The mooring ropes, taut as whips, trap
our feet. My friend tries to hook his carite,
but is cat-fish and cro-cro to throw back.

As the lone fisherman, meditative
at the end of the jetty, casts his lines,
frigates and pelicans soar above,
see what we don't see, bodies, floating crimes

among the plastic bottled detergents,
polystyrene foam cups, dragged by the currents.

East Coast
Manzanilla

The road is like old-time through cocoa shade.
Once I've left Sangre Grande's slow traffic,
cocoa pods, purple, yellow lanterns fade.
Villages crowd in with Soca music

till I hit Manzanilla's churned, brown surf:
the green interior of Nariva swamp,
Nariva River, the long Cocal's surge,
Radix Point and the brown Ortoire's slow slurp.

These are those mile posts on the heart's journey,
the beat of the ocean, beat of the heart.
Pujas prayed, garland the waves, while *jhandis*
fluttering from bamboo poles, erase the hurt.

With these and all other prayers I've counted
the murdered, those murdered, still more, murdered.

West Coast Macqueripe

After Mark Strand's "Blizzard of one"

They take their time and their love and drive out west
to see the setting sun, to feel themselves in this time,
to feel that time begin to leave them when the darkness
creeps to the edge of the blue-stone stairs descending
under the bamboo grove to the flooded beach. The repeated
waves beat out antiphonally their own time; then and then again
and then the swell and break of that green sea below

the immortelle's flame. They take their time and their love,
drive into the lights of cars towards the last blood
of the sunset, sit at their accustomed bar, drink
to their health and to the health of friends who
take their time and their love, sit out and wait
for their time and love to last, while others clink glasses
at other tables and the night has surely settled in.

North Coast
Maracas

The pelicans swoop for their evening fish
while the coconut palms walk to the sea
till morning sun when they rise again
to follow behind in the mangrove.

Rock pelicans! Sway palm trees! Vent Noel!
Blow Christmas breeze, sweet Maracas Parang!

While the sea's surf rolls in, breaks, hisses,
a ship's passage along the horizon
is our journey too till it disappears.
An atlas of clouds is also our map

of continents and islands and shadows.
Time flees these shades in search of their meaning,
old truths, that days turn themselves into nights:
spinning earth, revolving moon, static sun.

Tongues

In the swell, pirogues pull at the taut
moorings as tight as cuatro strings. You have
your heart torn by the old music in the names
of this coast: Maracas, Las Cuevas,
La Fillette, Blanchisseuse; the Spanish,
the French, in a patois made by Africa,

despite prohibitions, "Child, don't speak Congo."

An old-fashioned East Indian family,
a grandmother on the shore in her shiny dress
with her grandchildren speaks a tongue made
from *Bhojpuri* coming over the *kalapani*,
black water from Calcutta, Uttar Pradesh,

the canefields of Sainte Madeleine, Petit Morne,
the sugar-cane estate where I was born.

3
Town

Botanical Gardens

The trees that hold the early morning rain
drizzle as I pass under their dark shade
into the pale grey light which breaks through again.

Thunderheads, galloping fast behind, fade
off the Atlantic. The ground slips down
where the red-dirt track cuts through the bamboo

past broken steps under the pavilion
to the Botanical Gardens. An old taboo,
an old cruelty in the history,

rape, that quiet dawn, stabs with its cruel head.

A woman strolling in the last century
under a parasol of palms, unheard,
is the same woman jogging, her cries
stifled; the only screams, parrots' shrill shrieks.

Laventille
East Dry-River

Across this city is another country,
the hill, Calvary, climbing the Stations
of the Cross.
    Our Lady of Laventille,
Mother of youth, *Pietà*, as you look down,
your dead sons cradled in your lap, bleeding
from your arms, cry out:

> *five murdered today,*
> *five more gunned down yesterday, arming*
> *a police lock-down. Helicopter gun spray*
> *on the prowl circles the hill. Your gold diadem,*
> *a crown of thorns; your madonna's mantle*
> *laced with bullets.*

    What hope in prayer then,
in feet that beat the red-dirt yards, gentle
chant in the ganja air? In government?
Judicial corbeaux? Coins on the pavement?

Savannah Pan

January breeze: carnival. The ground moves.
Lamps lit in the surrounding hills above
bring the bands down from Laventille: Despers;
from up Saint James, Belmont, Woodbrook. Invaders
reach Savannah. Phase II Pan Groove on stage
below an immense sky, pan-moon. Steel rages:
stars hard as iron in the engine room; basins
of notes possessed by repeated lessons
beaten out on hot nights under galavanize.
Pan-yards transported. On the drag, peoples' lives.
Their eyes shine. The tin roofs glitter, jam
in half-lit darkness.
       Flash. Knife? *Pampadam.*
Is not a gun. Is not a gang. Wonder,
are the hands that beat the pans stained with blood?

Newtown

After Constantine Cavafy

What lives now in time is the memory
of them, where he stands under the street light,
Globe, Green Corner, languid, nonchalantly
waiting for a taxi that amber night.

But, catching his eye, as if by chance,
another stops and opens his door to him.
Smiling, he asks, 'You going Diego?'
In narrow streets where old aunts sang hymns

behind jalousies, saying rosaries,
they find an abandoned house. Above
the garden, over one of the balconies,
they cling; stars falling from the sky through a sieve.

The city's criers' cries travel on the breeze.
Even now, the scent of them is on their sleeves.

Lapeyrouse

August is a wall with frangipani
as pure as First Communion clothes,
the white of a wafer on the tongue, *oui*,
of a child of seven, whose small hands close
in prayer. The throat of the flower, tinted
with gold, is the chalice in a priest's hands
at a bowed consecration and tilted
to his lips. Sin is its sweet perfume and
a seductive breath by a blue-stone wall
in a town at night near Lapeyrouse, when
in the foreday morning after rainfall
the rain-flies lie dead. Their frail wings are then
smudges like moths' dust, ashes; Ash Wednesday
morning. After the *fête, Carne vale!*

Long Circular
St James

As the dusk comes down fast upon Saint James,
the lit lamps, constellations of fireflies,
dazzle, like Divali, Indian yards; flames
behind de Boissiere's house; children's cries.

Blowing another mood, the young college boys,
Q.R.C. uniforms, blue and khaki,
trumpet jazz into the saffron air, joy
from their young-fella yearnings, sighs

unbridled, standing in the police-barracks' yard,
as I drive by and yearn my yearnings too.
I take their blast, blown into the dark world,
mixing their brass like only jazz can do,

finding one tune in improvisation:
their melody, their hope, salvation.

Old-Time Port of Spain

For Nicky Laird-Paddington

While this time has sped and seems to have shrunk
to the O of this special decade's beginning,
I see the dawn light filtered over The Savannah
opening the jalousies of a young girl's room
on Sainte Claire Avenue, beckoning her to school
along the pitch-walk to leave her ginger-bread house
for the shade of pouis and flamboyante trees
as dew still wets the grass, while thoroughbreds
canter and gallop, groomed by young, lithe Indian boys.
The pedalling popsicle man rings out this time;
a call at The Dairies for hotdogs and sundaes.
It is the time when, even in older bodies,
the younger self is still eager for the future,
still has desire for that O in a moon: romance.

St Ann's
At Coblentz
For Marjorie Thorpe

As broad and deep as her counsel, laughter
filled the room, opening out from windows,
which framed the intimacy of chat; our
view of the hills painted with pouis, yellow
if the season, sprinkled with immortelle drizzle.
Alleluia, glory! Hymns, sung in Tunapuna,
later Donne and Herbert studied at McGill
she refined with our island's vernacular
through the rhyming couplets of calypso
as neighbourly as the roofs and streets in
Hinkson hung on her walls. She loved Shadow,
but *Sip and Chat* with rum punch her anthem,
as she made her home open house; above
all, embraced with an encompassing love.

Savannah

He watched evening: dun clouds, cobalt skies.
Or, like last night, seeing darkness grow
over The Savannah when the lights come up
on Queen's Park East, vermilion and lilac

burning like a cane-fire in the west
over the islands, the continental cordillera;
flambeaux burning round The Savannah
on oyster and boil-corn stalls,

ice-cold coconuts on Tony's truck
as the traffic circles and circles
under a full moon over Laventille
where you can climb Calvary:

but watch out for ganja-gun-shot,
police, and them with knives on the block.

4

Into The Hills

From Saddle Road

After Adam Phillips

i

An oriole startles the dawn with gold,
a ground dove taking me into the brown shade.
The last of the parrots fly in. Screams unfold,
while shadows skim the pitch road and rough verges fade.

Listen! A conversation: Schubert's fine strings
fill the room with frenetic dialogue, a frenzy
in *Death and the Maiden* quartet. Violins
fill the room with the birds going crazy.

Childhood solutions become the repetitions
of adulthood, a refusal to remember.
Memory is full of hiding places. Renditions
crackling with discordant sounds ensnare

these acute observations. Let them linger,
scratched by a bow: gut, steel, or, fine horsehair.

ii

This is the time of the singing frogs,
the early cock crow of betrayal.
This is the time of the singing tyres
on the Saddle Road back from a fête,

early market pick-ups weighed down with
crocus bags of onions and sive from the hillside
terraces of Paramin freighted into market.
This is the time with its mind on the North Coast

before the build up of traffic to Maracas;
and for me, how it must've been for him,
Cazabon, setting out before the hot-sun rose.
It is the same breeze, sky, mountains circling

the city, the harbour, the gulf he knew;
a sunrise tinted with pink turning orange.

Paramin

I did not know then what the pilgrimage meant
beyond the valley and the mountain climb
to Paramin. I wanted to hear *Crèche*
sung for Our Lady of Guadalupe
in a church that teeters on a precipice;
high above us the terraces growing
the sive, onions, tomatoes, lemons, limes.
On a stall at the church door: black coffee,
saltfish buljol, bake and sweetbread on sale.
An old faith in Trinidad fills a church
with cautro, guitar, drum and mandolin.
The women cry out, *Allez Mon Voisin...*

      As a songster sings in the breezy eaves,
      a black moth struggles at the pane with light.

On the Verandah

Now when the last cars speed by at night,
their swish drowning the music of the frogs,
I sit and listen to time's various beats:
a panist's ping pong, a lone man's night-time jog,
clatter of washing up, the tap's drip;
the beat of my own heart telling me
that at this time in this country minutes tick
by while loud voices blast, the bleatings weak,
following the brash message of ignorance,
of hate:'Hang dem high!' We hear them repeatedly,

while in the breeze at dawn's radiance
the wisdom of serpents, doves' humility
congregate, awaiting oriole's brilliance
blue jean's blue streak, the keskidee's
                              Qu'est-ce qu'il dit?

Maraval

When afternoons turn this calm and turn again
to dusks we know that are too tropic brief,
somewhere a yearning for summer evenings
remains where you are housed at home. My grief
grasps at moments while swifts still dart, and light
burns in braziers of bamboo clumps, palms move
their burnished branches to slow time. My plight
is to be here in this beauty that you've
known and you not part of it; in the day's sun,
now cooled by island breezes with night's approach.

While children's voices call, they want to remain,
Blake's nurse of *Innocence* lets them reach
for that extra play with no fear of dark,
no fear of the darkening savannah, the dogs' barks.

Scorched by dry season heat, cooled to dewy sweat,
I, John Thomas, bathe in the moon's chaste light.

Humboldt's Parrots

"There are moments in life when it is useless to call on reason."
Alexander von Humboldt: Personal Narrative Of Travels
To The Equinoctial Regions Of The New Continent, During The
Years 1799-1804

Blue-grey smoke like low cloud at dawn
climbs the dark, jade spurs above Maraval,
then slowly across the flanks, the steep cliffs,
trailing out towards the gulf, mercurial,
not yet fully lit: cloud, water, land
indistinguishable; another island,
continent stretched out on the horizon.

Despite the suburb of sky-scrapers I know are there,
I have that sense of standing on a shore
undiscovered, unexplored. Then, shocked
by my own thought, upbraided by the bush,
my seeming solitude becomes peopled, amplified;
Humboldt's parrots translating languages
into code: Taino, Aruac, Carib.

On Chancellor Hill
Of Parrots & Politics

i

A five o'clock walk in the afternoon
takes us away from Savannah's traffic,
takes us into bamboo shade's crac cric,
the tale of the parrots' roaring typhoon.

We are in a state of sudden elation,
not reckless. *You've checked the doors, the alarm?*
At the first bend the view is wide open:
islands, mountains, the gulf's charm;

an atlas of clouds, white scarves of Cirrus.
Then we climb on, translated by the light,
caravans of cumuli. We stop, cautious,
in awe of the valley, the summit's height.

On returning to our car, violence;
a socked rock, a smashed window, splintered glass.

ii

A fellow walker, coming towards me,
greets me with, *Venezuelan parakeets,*
boy! He presumes I do not know;
I am standing still and staring in awe.

I have known them from my birth. My brother
had one in a cage, a boyhood capture:
mongoose, agouti, manicou, squirrel.
I prefer the parrots' piercing rattle
in the wild, or, semi-wild of Chancellor,
rather than trained to mimic a master
in captivity.
              Megaphone orations
in the valley: the noise of politicians
block out the parrots with their vacuous rant,
kill the music with dangerous, racist cant.

Cassia Drive

It is now nearly winter in the north
and the days here begin to close early,
so it was a surprise to see his flight
across the half-lit sky's impending night,
transform the evening's aura into awe
of his presence which took its time to cross
the valley to the high trees above
the city to his eyrie, the dark limbs
of the tall cedars and mahoganies;
hawk, distinguished by his beak, that wing span,
that assured pace surveying all in fear
below, hopefully safe in their roosting branches.
We stopped and stared, watched him alight,
heard the rustle of feathers among leaves.

Full Moon Over Laventille

For N. L-P

I have little else now to give dear friend.
Walking out the other evening
on to The Savannah, I was astonished.
Just peeping out at first, a rim of light,
and then, as I began my circuit,
its full circle ballooned - a full moon!

I thought of you, that it was a sign
of wholeness and fullness, that
wholeness and fullness myself,
all your family and friends desire for you.

Whisked away, we miss you. Come back soon
through your cycles of pain and remedy.
Come back through the new stretches of time
you will have to live to come back whole;

circling the earth, a full moon over Laventille.

5

Departures

Boissiere Village

In a maxi-taxi through Boissiere,
schoolgirls in a huddle on their back seat
wave; the bright ribbons in their hair
like yellow butterflies in the wind. They greet
with smiles, laugh, tease, and playing with me
now you see me, now you don't. I smile,
wave back, feign hiding, duck my head, see
the littlest turning her head so, while
we play, play-play! So very refreshing;
driving through Boissiere in the hot
afternoon sun in the traffic, laughing.
Childrens' ecstatic freedom is their laughter,
their hide-and-seek, bright faces. Pretence
turns grotesque, dying with speed and distance.

Alamanda Court

Missing you, bereft of our familiar time,
I keep to our usual daily routines
where I fool myself I still find you, mine,
now that the surfaces are cleared of those signs:
lipsticks, lotions, perfumes, jewellery, scarves
tidied away, or vanished with your packed bags.
Two portraits stare at me, those years with laughs,
then ourselves now, old-age, when faces sag.
We have risked farewells before, interludes,
rehearsals for that final departure
when I, or you, will introduce the prelude,
the other present in the past's rapture,
to the final act. And then, that too will lapse,
present, past, future, fade away, collapse.

By the Pool

Where are you now, her letter asked, describing
September: the sky a vivid blue, autumn tints
bleed into the leaves. The elderberry's
fruit has ripened, the last of the roses blown
out like cabbages. She misses our walks around
the ponds at Parliament Fields, up Kite Hill
where we have looked at the sunset, the flight
of geese and been alarmed by swans landing
like Concorde.
        And here, when I, by the pool,
write and imagine her, my own evening
declines over the gulf, the palms; with the
shade of the calabash darkening, the last birds
on their last forays: this fallen leaf, a still life.

Dear Doro, in this light and from this distance now...

For Doro Baker

How to remember Doro from this distance,
in this light? What is distance and light *now*?
But then, on a sunny summer's day in Sutton
under a spreading apple tree, a round table
laid for luncheon with friends like family,
Doro and Hugh separate and inseparable:
Doro's radiant smile, Hugh, cavalier in Panama;
so much laughter with wine and Doro's good food,
making a family of friends in a *manor of thy friends*.
I remember her now: the counsellor of a pupil at our school,
her Irish tongue, the twinkle in her eye,
her moral strength, her salvo of political opinion,
the gentle, solicitous friend who sought me out
from among a family of friends for a one to one.

Mood of Departure

As the mountains fade into the late afternoon
in the haze which congeals on the Venezuelan coast,
the mood of departure descends upon the whole island.
The clouds bid you farewell as do their shadows on the plain.

The shade of the flamboyante is no longer necessary.
The egrets begin their return journey to the swamp.
It is the ending of the day. A saffron peace glows.
A cane-piece fire burns on the horizon beyond Patos

while the traffic melts down on the Churchill-Roosevelt
into that Saturday hustle returning from town.
I head west for home, an evening alone,
ti-rum on the verandah, the news and solo pasta;

head down early with the pillows, a novel's pages,
closing my eyes, the covers folding, falling to the floor.

Stillness

There is stillness now, conversation's ceased:
the talk in the head, the heart too full; each
bird call distinct against the blue distance;
the calabash in its own light, a green lamp;
the palms stilled in their sway to static fronds.
I begin a therapy of sonnets, these fourteen lines

keep me on a straight path, regular breathing,
all the way to the last couplet's resolution;
six lines to leave you waving good-bye at
the departure gate with your boarding pass.

All flight will alarm me for a day or two:
the egret's sweet benediction at dawn

followed by the parrots' hysteria; a troubled
pair screaming across the chasm of blue.

A Little Lent

For Jenny

She wrote of the autumn day she had spent
walking in the Chilterns with their close mates.
For a year now he had not had a scent
of that word, *Autumn*, wondered how it smelt.
She spoke of the soft light, which was filtered
through a smokey haze while *the winnowing
wind* kept a feel of that heat, summer-warmed
but with a hint of the cool damp evening.
And while that was it, she continued still
to describe the turning of the sycamores
and chestnuts. Their names terrified him, till
he had forgotten all of their colours,
consumed as he was by his own season,
Petit Carême; pouis, immortelles even!

Port of Spain to London

She tells me that it is grey and windy
walking on the heath. There's been a cold spell.
I tell her of the heat, the light, the blue swell;
the pirogue putting out, while she

tells me she misses our travelling selves.
I am all alone, *tout seul*, missing her;
sitting, like I do now, on the verandah
looking out to the horizon, to the one sail;

what we have made of our travelling,
taking me away, bringing me to home.
I'm no Odysseus, she no Penelope; oceans,
and what those journeys can do to people,

separations, the same as in the homecoming
as in life and in myths; scars and weaving.

6

London

Trapping Light
After Vermeer

Bereft of tropic light, he lays his traps,
lifts blinds at dawn, sets a strategic seat
this winter, on afternoons, at dusk, to catch
through the lattice of the cherry tree, slanting light.

He finds other traps laid: crimson berries,
a puddle, robin's breast, magpie feathers,
holly, ivy, laurel; silver birch,
where the wind, in all its wonder, gathers

light into the intimacy of a room
in Vermeerian yellow. His love
looks over her shoulder, not expecting him,
her eyes the blue above resounding surf.

At darkness, he looks into his heart
for warmth from the enclosure of her hearth.

On Parliament Hill Fields at Dawn

Was this my maybe future stretching ahead?
A single shadow strode the morning air,
you gone away, only to France, "Practising," she said,
ironically. "I'll need touch, to conquer fear,
whatever comes my way in this vanishing-game."
Yet a keen elation filled me as the light grew

sunrise on blades of grass, the weeping willow's mane,
vast circumference of the copper beech. A gull flew
up, circled once and then again became a tongue
of fire, which died as it settled on the water
in the mist rising from the surface of the pond,
not even a tremor on the fisherman's rod.

I move in my mind now between this new alone,
and my sense of you, alive, going south by train.

Still Life

After Chardin

A bowl of fruit on the kitchen table,
an arrangement of gladioli in a vase,
an orchid, moistened, kept in subdued light:
each to the passing eye is a still life,
caught in light the way, say, Chardin saw it:
still lifes whose plurals and singulars perplex.
We're still alive. We still live, and for this
we've planted a garden for our future,
water it day and night: fertilise, weed
and mulch. We've seen our flowers grow and bloom.
We've rearranged our house in which our lives
are still lived, in which our still lifes grow
and yet, in French, we are well reminded,
like nature, still life, translated, is *nature morte*.

7

Back To The Coasts

Lost Steps
After Alejo Carpentier's "The Lost Steps"

Walk now along the undulating ridge,
the ocean and the archipelago
to your left take you to Venezuela.
On your right, the valley undiscovered,
unexplored, not where you climbed from earlier.
Lit by morning light, caravans of cloud
drift out over the gulf: water, land, sky;
a Cazabon water-colour, *en plein air*,
fired by the sun. Descend the hidden stairs,
follow the red ribbons, take care, watch your step,
precipices left, deep chasms to the right.
The ground becomes a ladder to the shore as
we find *the lost steps* in the earth's sure holds;
then the embrace of the sea in Macqueripe Bay.

Grande Riviere

After Saint-John Perse
Image à Crusoe: La Ville

Heavy rains and the rough sea have broken
the sandbank of the swollen river, flood
mangrove and bamboo patch. Pirogues are moored
where the track once led to the wooden gate.
While the day has given Crusoe bright sun,
afternoon may bring sudden rain showers.
The sigh of the sea does not console his loss
nor the lapwing's inspection of the shore
find a solution to his old sorrow,
torn between his island's pull and London.
He sits and stares at the dark horizon;
a passing ship like a lit up city:
Crusoe's *cri de coeur*, '*O Ville sur le ciel!*'
is heard over the sands and the wet, slate roofs.

Moth Time

What is as still as time when a moth settles,
folding its wings as hands are folded
in prayer by a child's faith?
A moth on a leaf at the edge of the forest
is the hands of a clock at midday
and then again at midnight, folding time;
a moth with an eye on time, all-seeing time
which catches us walking upon an evening
in the blue of the last light which settles
like a mist on the green of the hills
over by Monte Video Zagaya and on the waves
in the bay of Grande Riviere,
all down the north coast to Chac,
to Venezuela. So far is time, so intimate, so far!

Bonasse Village

For Ken Ramchand

We walked the beach from Bonasse to Fullarton,
fishing villages at the end of the world,
an island on the edge of a continent,
where scabrous and scruffy shores fall into
the sea reformed by erosion. Islands come
and go in the channel, *Boca de la Sierpe.*
The sea's metronome tells a time of fifty minutes
from Bonasse village to Fullarton and back
along a shore alight with wild alamanda,
stories told by sedge and ferns in lagoons
fished for talapia and tarpon at Constance,
telling of former coconut estate gardens,
an *ancien regime* bred wild
in names like Agostini and Peschier.

Mayaro Love

For J.

I bring you nothing on this special day.
I had thought to have brought you the sunrise
but the *busie olde foole* beat me to it.
I had thought to have brought you bright, white sea-shells;
you could have them in abundance anyway,
that midden, the long beach rich with chip-chips,
star-fish, dollars. Plaited palms which the wind
had already designed for you? What then?
What can I bring you, you don't already have?
And even that I can't surprise you with.
Because you are certain of that I'm sure,
though doubt had crept years past. Dark horizons
now are merely weather. But, this no-thing
is what I bring, stealing the O from love.

Francis Trace

For Earl Lovelace

Dear Earl, I think how the years have passed now
since Jenny and I first drove up the coast
to visit you and Jean and the children, how
the country opened up for us. We parked just
off the main road, Francis Trace, still the sign
there, this year, where we stopped on the corner,
remembering with photographs that time,
lost and found. There is a new bridge over
the river, where the children fished for conchs.
There is that same dry-season breeze blowing:
fragrance in limes; the mango tree's branches
over the track to where the house stood leaning
into the forest.
                    We hold time in words,
listening to those voices from the yards.

"Green Days by the River"

After Michael Anthony

The yellowing river, the brown Ortoire,
flows reflectively in the khaki light
through cedar groves to reach the Atlantic
spilling over an ochre spit, witness
to the old quarrel between fresh water
and salt over a shoal of chip-chips gathered
by the tide. This afternoon, three fishermen
enter the channel in the pirogue, *Saint Michael*,
one steers the outboard, two in the belly
disentangle the seine. We have stopped by
the bridge to take this snap. They turn and stare,
lose their souls, they believe, not fighting this snapper,
keeping their eyes on their pull from the deep,
wondering at these interlopers who must capture time.

Laguna Mar

For Andrea

She slipped away in the night. We heard the news
by phone. Remembering her while the rain
falls this morning over the clouded hills,
we remind ourselves of that early morning call
choking us; and our tears for you dear friends,
husband and daughter, and for ourselves
without you, Andrea. It was hard to talk.

We took the death of our friend in our hearts
to the coast where the Marianne River
meets the green sea: and, as if knowing then
that she had died and what a wrench that was,
the sea convulsed swollen with a tide
flooding the wide beaches. Red flags were out;
on each white wave's breaking breath her name,

Andrea

Hingwan Style

(Edwin Hingwan, Trinidad artist, 1932-1976)

i

Looking through your coconut groves, Hingwan,
they lean towards the sea in your crippled style,
the trunks of coconut palms, their crowns twisted
back to the land by the wind, catching the sun.
Bright red pirogues, *Sea-Angel, Survival*, beached,
wait with the driftwood and dried weed in a tangle
of wild purple vine to be launched by four boys
who drag seine out to sea striding to the breakers,
the current pulling their net back to the beach.
All is tension towards the horizon between the shore
and the sea in the vast blue air on this wide
Mayaro beach, the surf repeating itself with a thud,
a hiss while your brush strapped to the back of your
hand paints the morning light that rusts the palms.

ii

Then, with the stroke of your brush,
the sky changes with a wash;
what was white with a tint of blue is now grey;
the sea before, green and frothy,
is the colour of zinc,
ripples like galvanize.
The seine this island pulls in
is stitched with needles of black rain;
in its net, a catch of silver
whose only future is a deluge.
The prayer of the cigale
has given way to the pinging frogs.
Once parched, we now regret our quenched thirst,
looking through your coconut groves, Hingwan.

Kernahan

iii

To reach the Cocal via Sangre Grande,
mist from drizzle lifting off the pitch road,
leave behind the smell of fresh, cutlassed grass
on the verge where the men used always to stand.

They cutlash, pause to sharpen their blades,
wipe the perspiration from their brows.
Then, have your vision altered, Hingwan style,
by the slanting light on the twisted palms

in ochre and yellow, or, rust and salt;
glint, dazzle, Atlantic Manzanilla.
A road sign, Kernahan, points to the swamp,
but the roar of the breakers turn you again

to where the light on water, spume and sound
break and break to the rhythm of the heart.

Atlantic

iv

Here, on the east coast, Mayaro beach,
Manzanilla fringed with manchineel;
bays and beaches alliterate
the names of their Amerindian ancestry,
while the Atlantic rushes in on the wind,
breaking repeatedly beneath a trinity of pelicans,
under almond trees, seagrape, coconut palms.

The sandpiper skitters on stalky legs in the surf,
foraging for food in the folds of the sand;
a mosaic of starfish and chip-chip shells.
Then, some dead thing alerts us,
a stingray, a giant from the deep,
beached, lodged in the weed,
pecked at by a caucus of corbeaux.

8

Up The Islands

Roseau, Dominica

For Polly Pattullo

In her father's, Dr Rees Williams', house in Roseau,
Cork and Queen Mary Street corner,
                              ghosts stand at the window.
Beyond rusty roofs, *mornes* like iguanas
climb into the blue. He climbs the steep stairs,
his hand upon the pitch-pine banister.
He clasps Jean's wrist as he is here to register
his allegiance, holding where she held on;
fingers within fingers that hold a pen,
turn an ocean's engine into waves that plunge
a green sun into Sargasso, make it orange
with a sunset whose rays fire the air;
a torn lace veil, as she retells Jane Eyre;
burns the Empire to the ground with this light
that lights the room with words she learns to write.

Guadeloupe
After "Fêter Une Enfance" - Saint-John Perse

Words are a world: hers, muslin for dresses;
linen for sheets and shirts; cotton for bodices
in *broderie anglaise*. He wears a pith hat
with a wet rim of sweat; carries a switch,

reins in hand, arms the colour of a mule,
his khaki sprinkled with ash;
his horse, Prudence. She dips her comb
in a glass of water, running it through her hair,

curling light; a humming-bird's hover, a halo.
She smells of *l'herbe-a-Madame-Lalie*,
yellow-white-lily-flower on a green
lawn collected by a black woman

with breasts of ginger. Bay rum on a hanky,
she pats the fevered brow of a white child.

Georgetown
Demerara

After Cazabon & Hippolyte Hartmann

The still, white town stares at the high seawall.
It does not see the brown waves, the sand banks,
the long jetty, the dykes, the coast going on and on.
It stares into the white glare and the steeples glimpse
the horizon. This is the Atlantic, that way to South America:
Suriname, Cayenne, Brazil. A brown arm points at
the canals, the turrets. The Dutch gables look back
at another horizon; a green light going on in a forest
beneath an immense sky. The domes bow in the sun.
The lighthouse looks down Water Street; it does not blink.
The boats arrive at the Demerara Stelling from upriver;
the interior disgorges its food at Stabroek Market.
a water-colourist and a photographer set up their tripods;
The pace of the 19th century is caught in lithographs.

Martiniquan Jazz

After Marley
&
"At the end of the small hours..." Aimé Cesaire's Cahier...

The moon's bright lip kisses the humming night;
its radiance illuminates the sea,
a path to the end of darkness, to light
up our love and bring you to me.

While down on the bay a jazz singer sings
of sorrow at losing his woman,
his tune, on the air, is a lover whistling.
A saxophone moans its own lamentation

where the sound of the waves on the rocks
is the tide pulling at the weed below
where the bright fishes glide and a keel knocks
hard against the jetty. I sway and go

down to the sands, pause, pick up the tune
of love and loss. As the singer joins Marley's
anthem, *No woman, no cry*, I look for the moon
in your face, in this night's jazz lullaby.

9
The Migrating Day

With acknowledgement to Richard Ffrench
For Pat Rigg & Jane McIntosh

i Dawn

The pale clouds, before they are lit fully by the morning sun,
peal off into the white flight of white egrets from the swamp.
There is a single seraph, then pairs, threes and fours,

a flock, blessing the green valley with benedictions
of peace and quiet, despite the swish of early morning traffic
on the Saddle Road; blessings upon houses which climb the hills

and spread along the valley floor. The summits of the mountains
are first to be lit, then the light gradually descends to erase
the shadows where ground doves feed, shadows on walls,

where the bougainvillea falls in avalanches of purple,
vermilion and white. In that growing heat, the frenzy,
the scatter and scream of the first migration begins.

Parrots, bursting out of jade forests, catapult themselves at speed
across the morning skies, now a growing cobalt. Egrets' wings
are clouds again, now tinted with blush, orange and dun.

Parrots whose flight is a furious flapping of pairs upon pairs
join their flock as they scatter, landing on the high trees;
on the bamboos in the gulches of green, dried out

in the ravines of stone and moss; on rivers dried up.
Sun lights the rock face from where the parrots have torn
their green light that sparks yellow under their wings.

The flight across the valley takes time to settle,
to weigh down the branches of the feeding trees,
to nestle into the flowering crowns of the tall-tall palmistes,

to peal off the bamboo's tender shoots. These migrations
of parrots are startled by the chasms of air, the vaults of blue.
They scream and scream and scream, till they settle and feed.

ii Morning

The morning grows as hot as a kiln;
the tanagers continue to feed.
Their flight is a streak of blue,

the green of palm, the russet
of dry leaves, the colour of tanned leather
where it curls like in ancient archives

of forest stories; documents of seasons.
Tanagers, with white stripes, silver beaks,
startle the ordinary, making the keskidees' questions,

Qu'est-ce qu'il dit, monotonous and too yellow.
The sleek, black tanager, is a black almost purple.
An oriole's yellow is an epiphany of gold

with a single call to follow its shy disappearing flight
from the red bottle-brush tree,
darting through hedges of alamanda.

iii Noon

By midday, the corbeaux have sway in the high thermals,
a god-like view, a vulture's search for carrion;
the binoculars of a bird on the dry world:

the parched plain, the bush fires in the hills,
the metallic gulf, the haze building and piling
up on a horizon as far as Venezuela,

erasing the cordillera that runs
the spine of the continent.
Our Andes is on fire!

Close by, an osprey on a dry branch,
is startled in its solitude where it too spies its prey,
talapia, in the last dregs of a sunken pond in a burnt pasture.

The air is clogged with a dust
as red as Sahara sand,
wind as strong and dry as the Harmattan.

The air and wind sing with the perpetual engine
of the cigale's cicada throbbing in this heat
beating a hot pulse under the sweating temples.

iv Afternoon

The sun is on the other side;
the verandah is in shade.
The tanagers are here for a second feed

on the left-overs of the morning;
banana skins blackened by the sun, rotting
pawpaw skins as fine as the skin of a skinned rodent

fester. Cups of grapefruit and orange,
are dried pulp dredged of all their juice
drunk in the morning. They crawl with ants.

v Dusk

Between the shadows and the last of the hot light
the migration, the return, begins from this side of the valley
to the hills above The Savannah. Like clockwork,

a mass departure rises up out of these hills,
moving in pairs, in furious, flapping multitudes of pairs
with all the screams they have saved up all day.

The flight of green light
settles among the bamboos,
flamboyantes, cocorite palms.

The shade and shadow of a fast increasing evening
smells of the earth that has yearned for shade,
smells of the juice of hot plants yielding their perfume,

herbal scents and rich fragrances; chadon beni, wild mint
reek and leak into the hot air; a sweat excreting itself.
The whiff of wild animals reaches the road

as they cross in search of water in the dark.
An agouti is a migration of dry leaves
through the fading light into the darkness.

vi Night

It has suddenly descended,
though, if you climb the hill to the old forts
and look out over to the other side of the coast,

there is a fire burning out its orange,
its red furnace. Its flame and flare
light up the coastline from La Fillette to Chacachacare.

The birds have left the world to the music of frogs,
unless you are at the water's edge in that last light
to see the last frigate bird soar over Gasparee,

out towards Monos and the fading archipelago.
The motor of a single pirogue brings in a lone fisherman
through the darkness across the oily water to the jetty.

The jumbie bird, the pygmy owl, is all eyes.
Its hoot-hoot tells us that other safaris
begin in the forests: sonic bats, screech bats,

the oily guacharo, the common pootoo.
They hunt till first light. Sleep is a drone
through the cool of El Tucuche in the air-conditioner.

As I wake to the distant barking of dogs
up the valley, there is the intermittent swishing speed
of a late-night-early-morning-car.

I dream of parrots and their migrations.
The silent ridge is silhouetted against a mauve sky.
If you wake and go out onto the verandah,

you'll see Paramin's mountain lamp-lights like stars;
the moon, the night's sentinel. You'll hear
the jumbie bird, the night caller,

over the drip of condensation;
the night's cold sweat,
falling on to the cooling pitch.

Literary Biography

Lawrence Scott's most recent novel is *Dangerous Freedom* (Papillote Press, March 2021). In the same year, his first novel, *Witchbroom*, was translated into French, *Balai de Sorcière* (Mémoire d'Encrier, 2021) by Christine Pagnoulle (Liège University). His second collection of short stories, *Leaving by Plane Swimming Back Underwater* (Papillote Press, 2015) was longlisted both for the Edgehill Prize and the Frank O'Connor Short Story Award in 2015. His novel, *Light Falling on Bamboo* (Tindall Street Press, 2012, Profile Books, 2013) received an honourable mention from Casa de las Americas Prize, Cuba, 2014; was longlisted for the International Impac Dublin Literary Award, 2014; a special mention from the Grand Prix Littéraire de l'Association des Ecrivains de la Caraïbe from the Congrès des Ecrivains de la Caraïbe, Guadeloupe, 2013; it was shortlisted for the OCM BOCAS prize fiction category, and longlisted for the overall OCM BOCAS Prize, 2013. His second novel *Aelred's Sin* (1998) was awarded a Commonwealth Writers' Prize, best book in Canada and the Caribbean, longlisted for the International Impac Dublin Literary Award, 1999, and longlisted for both the Booker and Whitbread Prizes, 1998.

His first novel *Witchbroom*, 1992, was shortlisted for a Commonwealth Writers' Prize, 1993, Best First Book, and read as a BBC Book At Bedtime, 1994. His first collection of short stories *Ballad for the New World* (Heinemann, 1994) included *The House of Funerals* which was given the Tom Gallon Award, 1986. His novel, *Night Calypso*, 2004, was also shortlisted for a Commonwealth Writers' Prize, best book award and longlisted for the International Impac Dublin Literary Award, 2005, and translated into French as *Calypso de Nuit* (Sabine Wespieser Editeur, 2005). It was a "One Book One Community" choice in 2006 by the National Library of Trinidad & Tobago. He was the editor of *Golconda Our Voices Our Lives*, an anthology of oral histories and other stories and poems from the sugarbelt in Trinidad (UTT Press, 2009). Over the years, he has combined teaching with writing. He lives in London and Port of Spain. He can be found at www.lawrencescott.co.uk.

Acknowledgements

I acknowledge quotes in my epigraphs from Derek Walcott's *Another Life* and from Wilson Harris's *The Music of the Living Landscape*. I also acknowledge quotes from Adam Phillips in the sonnet, "From Saddle Road i". I acknowledge quotes from Saint-John Perse, Aimé Cesaire, John Keates, John Donne and Bob Marley. I wish to thank Mimi Khalvati for her sensitive response and sound advice; Lorna Goodison, Robin Robinson and Mervyn Morris for their encouraging words. I also wish to thank Polly Pattullo, at Papillote Press, for her generous-hearted support over the years, her tireless efforts and sensitive editing. My collaboration with her for this publication has been as enriching as our previous involvement in the publication of three of my prose works. I wish to thank Andrew Hewson, my agent at Johnson & Alcock, for his encouragement and being a dear friend over many years. Jenny Green, as always, has been a constant reader, listener and sharp critic. Nothing happens without her during 50 years of a life together.